Seasoned

Edson Burton

First published 2009 by City Chameleon
82, Colston St,
Bristol,
BS1 5BB

ISBN 978-0-9551180-4-3

A CIP copy of this book is available from the British Library

Designed by City Chameleon
Cover designed by kambendesign
Printed by Short Run Press

Seasoned is the culmination of years of writing and refining since I first came to Bristol. The people and sights that have informed me are too numerous to mention so I apologise in advance for those who I have not mentioned but I would like to thank, in no particular order, Bertel Martin (City Chameleon) for years of support and indefatigable patience, Tom Phillips my editor, Helen Dunmore, Bristol Black Writers, Eastern Can Openers, Say It Loud, Grace, Reuben, the Burtons, Dores, Ruth, my school teachers Mr Leech & Mr Lind for support beyond the call of duty, Katy, Sam Berger, Tanuja, Rob, Miles the George Bell Institute, Madge Dresser, Melroy, Vida, Marc, Sue, Victory Park, Snuff Mills, all the rivers, mountains, lakes that have spoken to me my ancestors known and unknown.

Edson Burton
2009

Acknowledgements
Song of the Ghanaian Coast c/o of Breaking the Chains exhibition Empire and Commonwealth Museum Bristol.

Contents

Song of the Ghanaian Coast

Go ka Nu Dze G Woyinka
Go ka Nu
Adose kple Afedima Woe Yina Dua
Adose kple Afedima Woe Yina Dua
Go ka nu Dze Ge Woyinka

On which shores are we going to land?
On which shores are we going to land?
On which shores?
There go Adose and Afedima far away.
There go Adose and Afedima far away.

On which shores are we going to land?

Exile

Ship

We lie,
Three deck and dying,
Eyes yawning, into a sky
Of rotting timbers.

Pressed close in putrid darkness,
We form one foetal mass
Suspended in a shrunken womb.

Company provides no consolation.
Made mute by the talk of myriad tongues,
We suffer in isolation.

Dreams taunt and tune
The filth and stench of bodies
Into memories of sensuous life
Of colours and textures doomed
To libraries entombed within fading minds.
We long to witness the naked light.

We once human heaps
Burst into boils, pustules,
And seep life, like the sunlight
That breaks the brutal back
Of day.

Terror-worn, we wall in
The carnage that conquers the inner life,
And pray to diverse Gods
To grant death's blissful kiss
But as the spirit frees
The ship's rocking gentles,
The call of gulls is heard overhead,
The hatch opens
And our hearts wait
To break on new shores.

Seasoned

When you claim massa bran
As if it was bongo mark,
Clear forest, chop cane
Til yu sap run dry,
Come a night time
Nyam hog swill
Like it a sweet meat.
When yu bolt like boar
To be firs in de field
An backra han can
Fall pon de unruly
When yu see yu first born
Fingered on de auction block
An yu yeye water wid pride
Cause dem fetch good price.
When yu accept de stump
Where yu foot once fall,
As God punishment
Fa when yu did bawl
Bout freedom
Den African you are seasoned.

A Traitor's Heart

Tobacco-brown hands
Lift him high, arms fold
To form a cradle
Fingers curve along:
Full sallow cheek,
Corn gold curls,
Thin pursed lips.
He bears the imprint
Of a once helpless suckling
Grown stern and impudent,
Her 'lickle massa' nonetheless
Raised on her milk
While swollen-bellied picannies
Lowed like lost cattle in the fields.

She has woven every stitch
Of a blanket binding generations,
Surrendered a slave's yearning
In nurturing a dynasty's ambition.
Tonight this nocturnal habit
Holds the power of life and death.

The dark beyond, a feline black,
Is murky with mystery and malice.
Under its cover in the barracks
A plot is spun to breathe
Life to a dream none dare name.

She sees the day to come,
Sighs with awe and dread
This milk-white crest crowned
With blood, her quilt ripped
Torn ruined unless, by her
Word, a revolt is undone.

How Our Love Survives or The Lovers' Contract

If you hold me sewn with scars,
Heavy with the stench of the day's sweat,
Nor writhe at the touch
Of my whip-riven skin,
I will not dream of innocence.

If you take my hands, forever
Engraved by clawing at dirt,
Trace my lips blistered by cursing,
I will sweeten your soul soured by sorrow.

If you do not ask me to speak the secrets
Of my hated visits to the Great House,
Then I will caress your unspoken distress
On your return from the stables.

If you cast your eye to the earth
When I am chastised by the cat o' nine,
Then we shall meet again
To heal that space with kisses.

If you embrace the fullness of me
When I bend and scrape
To please and deceive Master,
I will be faithful to you
As you curry favour to avert hunger.

And if you or I are sold abroad,
Let us steal away on those Sundays,
Even if we have but seconds
Before sunrise speeds our divorce.

Let me clasp you,
Part and twine your locks
In wistful patterns that recall
The lanes and straits of our lost settlements.

Let us hum lullabies in our mother tongue,
Dance the delicate quadrille
And burst with laughter mocking Backra,
Weave tales of Anansi cunning.

Let us conjure the ocean-wide rivers,
Mist-crowned mountains, the moist melting forests,
The vast open plains of home.
Let me bathe in your words.

Prize me, as I you, when we are not precious.
Push me like life newborn back into the World.

Spring

I

I see her for the first time:
A scarf of skin over jutting bones
A solitary tear for lost ones
Living an act of iron will.
And know she is my soil.

II

Dazed by owning his own self
He stoops as if still scourged.
Bends an ear to earth for warnings.
My love will straighten him.

III

My first recall: milk and smuggled meat,
Acrid scent, weary sigh,
Horn blow, his curses, her kiss.
Chunks of green in their absence
Alone. Pecking at the dirt.
Now they are faces, fingers
A limp, a skip, a sudden snarl
Smiles. Spirits that I learn to know.

Eucharist

Hunters poised before a throng
Stand astride their prey
Frenzied stare and foaming mouth
Speak the rapture of the hunt.
Infants in sharp- eyed wonder
Like cherubs at a hellish feast
Perch upon blistered branches
To gorge upon every morsel.
The prey: lashed to the cotton tree
Brown body charred black
Terror twisted stare, spine
Snapped by the killing rope,
Balls and all, rammed down his throat,
Is served up like a communion wafer
Before a grisly Eucharist.

Job

Job's fingers press inwards
Forming a bible arrowed upwards
Its black cover the black backs of his hands
His bones its bindings
His palms its psalms
His lines engraved gospels.

Job's cracked lips press close.
Cave dark eyes clam up.
He prays for another skin
In which God will, surely,
Love him.

Job hears only the hum
Tastes only the brine
Of his own cries
While God incarnate suffers
And falls, within his tears.

What Stella Didn't See When She Got Her Groove Back

She swelters under intense admiration
As suitors like satellites in broken orbit
Queue eagerly for collision
Far cry from home:
Unobtainable
Unavailable
Homosexual.

In time her star aligns
With a fellow Gemini:
With him she is four
Marvelling at rock pools
Sixteen tasting a melon-tinged
Kiss.
Grown - dripping in a post-coital cascade

She paints upon the sky canvas
Candles tensing, melting
Soft-focus family gatherings
Confetti, parenting.
She resolves
To take him home.

But he too has dreams
Beamed daily into the rum shop
A soft bed and secure sky
Cooled air indoors
Karl Kani, Versace
Kentucky, Miss Millys
Fast food, frozen food
24 hr chat freak shows
The beamer bouncing to
Thumping basslines
Finally to discard his rustic charm
With razor-sharp education.

Stella
And
Celestine
June
Leo
Juanita
Brigita
Ling
Lara
Are prims
Through which he consumes paradise.
Their ease a seasonal reprieve
From ceaseless anxiety.

This escape was enough
Until the proposition was made.
Stella did not see his hesitation
The clink of rapid calculation
The tinkle that mesmerized ignite
With a furious light his
Nonchalant smile turn servile
Her dreams converted to a commodity.
Stella does not see that stars
Do not shine on cloudy nights.

The Old Slave Market

Dispersed among the arches
We wait like hungry wolves
Sat in the squares centre
The griot strums a plaintive song.

They come, clumsy colourless
The griot hisses subtle seduction
They turn over and over, inspect
Our wares, haggle, barter, bully
Laugh feebly to our native smiles
Express shame for ancestral crimes
Pose for holiday snaps.
Leave.

All day in the heat
The endless repeat
The griot's elegy
Turning to summons
Calling the children on.

But as the air thins
As the light dims
Shadows lengthen into human shapes.
We hear the clank of chains
Growls and groans
Near-animal cries in ancestral tongues
The stink of fear and fresh branding
We must not stay.
The griot remains
To give lost souls solace.

Hate Crime

It is not the bellies of ships crammed with Black bodies, like berries,
to be crushed for wine.

It is not the tumult of bones lining the bottom of oceans of the living
and dead cast overboard.

It is not the coarse valleys carved into backs by whips unfurling like
vicious tongues.

It is not the legion of dream-drunk minds wasted waiting for an
afterlife.

It is not the sight shrunken to horizons cane and cotton field high.

It is not the death of tender words drowned by the regime's mighty
roar.

It is not even the memory of showing mercy through infanticide.

The enormity of the crime was teaching me to hate the mirror.

The Great House

I look up at the Great House
Its beacon light blazing
Through the darkening canefield
Pause and ponder its fineries.

I look up at the Great House
As its moon like light
Mocks the flinching flame
That illuminates my studies.

I look up at the Great House
Its sight anaesthetising
The aches of another day
As I return from the factory.

I look up at the Great House
To revive my lost verve
After hours spent rote-learning
Legal writ.. Restored I return.

I look up at the Great House
As my will begins to wilt
After hours spent memorizing legal writ
Its sight restores the celebral switch.

I look up at the Great House
Through the smoke and din
Of celebrating a day's verbal brawling
And know I pave my approach.

I look across the Quay
At the sprawling estate
Beyond and below
And am by a vision gripped.

Steel pipes, tiered scaffolds
Rise from the gaping hole
- the estate bulldozed.
I await entry to my Great Home.

Forward

Come man come
Even if you get qualification
You nar go be someone
Yu complexion wrong, wrong
An yu people ave no connection
So I beg yu, please come.

Nuh believe story of milk an honey:
Life no easy, people wuk like machine
Winter time it so col yu skin scream
An de English is de strangest people yu cyan meet.

Still dis is a lan of opportunity
Come nuh man mek big money
An when yu done yu cyan go
Ome an buil up we country.

Ere de oman a fall like pear from tree
An all dem wan pick is we
It no even matter weder yu black or ugly
- Mi know yu ave yu honey -
But come nuh ave a lickle fun wid me.

So nuh tarry book yu passage
When yu come bring bottle a rum
Bring news of de family
An dem bwoys dem, Defreitas,
Coolie man John
Bring mento record
If you can bring piece a yam
Bring piece a ome.

Exodus

Tired

Mouse-quiet mi crawl
Under her zzzzs
Warm water wash
Two pails pick up.
Ease in de door.

Nod to granny
Headstone. Tru de yard.
De fores is steam
Risin under sun cross yeye.
Curtain of mango
Red as dusk mark mi pat
Mi foot fall pon overripe paw paw.
The spilt sap feedin
A million little ones
Waitin pon de fores floor.
Leaf tun lizard
Lizard lick ant
Straight off de bark
An two orange back beetles
A make life pon a branch.
Mi want fe still
But no time to idle.

By de river side
Mi part fever grass
Step over vine
Ben an polish de potatoes
Bright like church chalice.
Stagger back up de bank.
One pail full a yam an one a water.
Nuh spill a drop.

Roun de belly
Under de bump
De spud a sick white man
An mi a top surgeon.
De soup on: mi press, mi iron.

She foot drop like thunder
Full awake like hunter
She shake off slumber.
"Ahem." She lift de lid
Sips... The worl stan still.
She lay de strap
Woun roun she fist
Down, down, down
Pon she bed.
Praise God.

II

Inglan
A gray brew
Heavy like mudder
But de emerald hue
Is familiar an new.

Inglan a new dance
But mi tired already.

Long Way From Home

Mi is a West Indian,
Upright Anglican,
Come fe bring mi medicine
For war battered Inglan.
An to prove we is de equal to anyone.
Mi fin a wuk as a conductor
pon bus 71. Mi smile wid everyone
No matter if dem miserable.
Every face an diary
Mi know like de back a mi han.
Mi fix up my voice an manner
Fe imitate a true Inglish gentleman.
Den one day, mi buk up pon dis
Ol oman a sey nah pay a damn.
She would rader go prison
Dan touch mi monkey, monkey han.
She call mi a black shite an
Repeat it an repeat it an repeat it.
Mi search fa a saviour: all mi see
Is a sea of broadsheet.
Dats when mi lose mi
Grip and give she
One big lick.
Is den mi realize
How far mi is from home.

The Ark

He opens the peeling trunk,
Plunges into history.

She eyes the open trunk,
Symbol of downward mobility,
Pot of infidelities. Black bin liner open and ready.

'Dat dey trunk belong inna de dump.'
'Gwan lef mi no oman mi will sart it out.'

Boarding pass on Esconia
Recall chill Atlantic squall
And the warmth of expectation.
Crumpled trilby once
Entry to Bogart fantasy.
Zoot suit pressed
To pencil-sharp perfection
Summon illusions of opulence
On seven bob an' ten.
He reels 'Man l could fancy me'
Frozen in celluloid smooth skin,
Eyes fixed on the future.

He feels the razor edge.
Letter from Pearl:
'Greetings in the name of Jesus.
'When yu a come home?
'Will yu send fa we?
'Let the children know
'Dem have a Daddy.'
The razor still washed in tears.
The return pass - 1963 -
Still sealed.

Flask and chipped coronation
Mug, gold watch hands stopped.
Splotched boiler suit mark
Thirty years' service
To the foundry.

Rum bottle reeks memories
Fierce nights in hazy domino halls.
Ah, Coolie John, now where's he?

Elfin winklepickers'
Gaping heel, revive
Marcia and he joined
Hip and cheek
In a backstreet shebeen
Bluebeat grinding before Jesus intervened.
Father Christmas on a card
Memento from Irish Mary.

Vinyl graveyard lies buried,
Coiffered Jim Reeves on a torn cover,
Quiet Sundays crooning with Nat King Cole,
Hypnotized by half-recalled chords,
He blows away dust clinging
To the magical vinyl.
'My baby jus' cares for me.'

'Enough sartin fa now.'
Another time maybe.

Shango

The bridge ascent is your Everest,
Each step a landslide
Of agony to arthritic knees.
We pause for the pain to let up.

Below, the dead factory:
Rust and weed hedged
Hollow: giant bird's nest.
Cold kiln of memory.

You smile cryptically:
Extract, laval heat,
Frenetic drama,
Iron order.

But smelting
Joints of industry
Returned to me
To me a crippled shade.
Conned by Christmas
Pantos, stale chocolate,
Santa's rum wet beard,
The gold watch a fool's Holy Grail.

You rub my hair:
Comforted by lineage:
I plot class revenge.

What Is Jamaica 2 Me

My father's isle in the sun
Home of bird and canecutter's song.
Land of peace and love
And M16s at every turn.
Land of Rasta utopias and urban hells
Of homes made, and undone
By the flight of daughters and sons.
Land where playboy ostentation
Mocks desperate aspiration.
Land of endless ease and restless hustle
Of shebeens and bacchanals by the sea.
A perfect mission field and epitome
Of Victorian hypocrisy.
Land of church bells and Kumina drum
Of a million Romeos and dreadlocked gigolos
Of child mothers and infant men
Land of peasant dignity and rural poverty.
A melting pot and nation fragmented
Land of new technology, yet where spirits dwell
In the green glow of fireflies.
Well from which I draw.
All this and more is Jamaica to me.

Orpheus and Eurydice

Orpheus how deep will you descend
Into Eurydice's hell? Locked
Pacing her padded cell
Shrieking at a vacant screen.
Playing with her excrement
As an artist would with a pen.

In the lift of opiate like love
You crafted covenants
That outshone the pompous sun
That brought proud eros to envy.
But to what end now she is numbered
Among the living glazed?

Upon your gilded promise
She became a nymph rising,
Like an aria from earth's origin,
Upon melodies sprung from your majestic heart.
But will you catch her when she falls
From grace, her euphoric state
Turned into a trance of hate?

If offered an escape
In clinical persuasions
Would you take counsel
Or wage sedition against her sedation?

And if sharing her fate
Sullied the music that
Soothed the most savage breast
If you too risk madness
Will you cast off this love
Only to revisit its sweet bitter memory
When scavenging food for poetry?

Is Eurydice your muse
From which your lyricism flows
Or does your soul see no further
Than its own imago?

Orpheus how far will you descend into Eurydice's hell?

Naked

You are without borders I without hidden quarries
By familiarity we have leave to roam freely
The parched earth of sorrow in the wake of evaporated hopes
The frozen hatreds that form like glacial clots upon an arctic flow
The mist of doubt that thickens into cotton thick fog
The flutter and dart of desire like cells racing to unknowable ends
Loch clear lucidity in surrender to unstoppable deluge
The tumble of thoughts varied like life in jungle canopy
The shadowy depths of mysteries into which we cannot see
Naked thus are we now too coy to touch.

Homecoming

Had you but paused
To take in the wide
Hungry eyes waiting
For Grace to fall
If you had bent
Encircled soothed
Let a soft word fall
If you could have felt
The pitch of that moment
Seen the crater formed
By your plummet
But you could not echo
Words never uttered perform
Mercies never bestowed picture
Images never drawn. And the One
Above did not grant the Gift
To divine the Unknown
You are the bloodline:
Unmarked canecutters,
Higglers, homeweavers,
A mother who passed
Before her milk would come
Bequeathing to a sobbing girl
A sibling brood
And a soured childhood.
I scream the cut
Tumble and crash
Upon the abrasive ground
Of my own cells
And know that I am alone.

Vessel

Commitment Phobia

Your green fields
Emerald forests
Moonlike moors
Clear and murky waters
Are all I have known
Yet I cannot commit.

I have warmed
To your bipolar passions
That defy all forecasts
Yet I cannot commit.

Abroad, I have longed
To churn butter-soft soil
To kick leaves, crisped and crinkled
On a clear morning
Yet I cannot commit.

Through you I have accrued
The tongue, ear and eye
Of every continent.
Yet though giddy with gratitude
I cannot commit.

I cannot commit
For although I am a native son
Yet still am I looked upon
As an exotic doll
Eternally newly come.

I cannot commit
For my journey to you
Has been built upon
A long-lived duping
And I tremble with rage and shame.

I cannot commit
For your slash and burn love
Permits only my loss.
And your victory the only outcome.

I cannot commit
So I disgrace citizenship with satire
Find Zion's in untested scholarship
Retreat into self-centric parody.
But you are the drunken steward of our ship
Upon your course our fate is sealed.
Unless I too turn the wheel
We shall both perish upon the rock.

IC3

Things that are good in nature think on these

But Lord forgive me
My wit's diseased
And the most diseased
Thing on this earthly tree
Is me.
Poisoned by
Eyes scooping me like CCTV
Seeing me as they see me.
Just anotha IC3.

Gold tooth grin and nuff bling bling
Riding a riddim of rob and ruin.
Psycho driven engine
On collision with prison.

Escape the pen,
Fly to outer city heaven
But here civility doesn't extend to me -
Curtains rustle, strangers jellify
When I pass by -
Here I am a refugee
Or yardie from the inner city
Accused by their fantasies
Tried by the Beast,
If I'm lucky, or Neo-Nazis.
Found guilty of being
Just anotha IC3.

I turn to Christ
But can't see past the idolatry
His cold blue eyes
Staring down on me.
I turn to the SWP
But they tell me
I'm just anotha IC3
Only with a touch of sympathy.

'It's all in your head
Get that chip off your shoulder'
The system says.
But don't be misfed
Believe that B/S
And walk the street like Night of the Living Dead
Pumped, pumped, pumped
Full of lead.
Every city has its broken army of IC3s.

So much chaos inside
Sometimes I think I've already crossed the line.
But I won't let it happen to me
Cause I know there ain't no care in the community.

My career adviser
Deals the cards for me:
IC3 or Zombie:
'Minstrel a la MTV'
'Smack n crack dealer'
'Serial babymaker'
A cog in the machine:
Ah the Euro-American dream
Head down
Uttering empty
Work, work, work
Weekend burst
A holiday in Ayai Napa
And when you're downsized
Rationalized
Denationalized
Collect your state money
And wait for the New Deal.

So hard to hold
Onto positivity
To flip the script
Written for me
So hard just to be
Just to be, to be, to be.

Champion

Gloved in cold fury
Bell rings. Unhinged.
The boy is slick
Cuts in leans out
Ducks and disappears
Grins.

Too cocky
Up thrust chin
Smash. The jolt is pure joy
Shock he can't hold in
Wounded he rallies.
Now we begin.

Rapid fire
Rights lefts
Bang, bang, bang
Caught clean.
Judder. Clench
Wait out the barrage.
In a contest of wills
I am without compare

Heads crash. Blood
His. I slash and slash open
Wide the gash beyond
Corner man miracles.

Shuffling in panic
Auto pilot
Out of tricks
Could end it quick.
But gonna punish that grin:
Dismember him.

Stab deep into the ribs
Hands move down
Head meets my
Hurricane hook.

A feint - call him in.
Snap him back
Jab, uppercut and elbow
In the clinch
Whisper bitch, bitch, bitch.

Up on instinct
Gloves waves feebly
Legs leaden, body
Leans against mine
Light as papier maché.

Like a master butcher
I probe, probe, prise out the prime
Cuts kidney, heart, chin.

He slides slowly down
Lies stretched across
The stained canvas
Black body bruised
And glistening.

Stand over him.
Champion.

Dawg Lover

Mi ave a dawg me no keep pon a leash
Mi ave a dawg dat nuh ave nuh teet
Mi an mi dawg is join in matrimony
When mi a dey a res me dawg sleep pon me ches
Me dawg belly full but it always hungry
Mi and mi dawg nyam pure pedigree
Man love mi dawg but no dem no fe touch ee
You nar see me dawg if yu nuh pex me
But if yu mix up inna my business min:
When me dawg bark it open ches cavity.

Smile

Don't blow no kisses
Dis ain't no Mills n Boon
Turn off the r'n'b tune
Dis aint getting to know you.

Arse up hands and knees
Leave on dem heels.
Work you like a whip
Stretch you like a wire
Beat on you wid dis dick fist
Till you submit.

Love de clap clap when
I smack that, way dem ripples
Sizzle, when your skin
Glistens, de riddim of dem
Phat nipples. If I had a shank
I'd make an incision.

Fuck, shit I'm gonna bust
-No hold back, get the camera,
Record my own skin flick.
Tun round choke on dis
Taste dat seed bitterness
Don't swallow let it drip
Let it drip.

Look at the camera.
What dust in your eye?
Smile. Smile. Get off my sheets
You stink like a slave ship.

Time for me to shower
Gonna call my spars;
The night's still young:
Dey can all get some.

Young, Gifted, Dead

Rigid black lies
Upon ungiving grey
Liquid red seeps pulped
Cartons irrigates cracks
Twitching rats count
Down his last breath.
Clubbers congregate
Iridescently undressed,
Their curious chatter his eulogy
A siren's wail his requiem,
A weary sigh his last post
Announcing his epitaph:
He was young gifted and dead.

The Kiss of Life

You were wrought at the point of vicious intent
Born despised and kept in darkness
Exposed to forge distance from the faint-hearted
And to make solidarity with brute-loving men
You became an oracle for those who would divine.
But now in late years reveal your true substance.
Scar, you are the rose rising
From the bloodied crossroads between
Rage, calm, chaos and creativity
A kiss of life brought by a knife.

Choke

Marooned

1
Caught by your smile wide
As an eagle's wingspan
Your tight tidy kinks
Smooth nutmeg shine
Your wit when I test
Your catlike composure
You carry your mother's care.
Crop of home you I long to taste.

But you
Pass
Pass
Pass
Pass
Me by on your way to another
Why?
Ain't I a woman?

You play with me in the awkward hours
When wine and night become narcotic
But will not stay a while.
I take the booby prize
Find warmth in men who
Leave my core cold.
You turn away as if I am defiled.

2
You are the rainbow
Of brown, mango
Round, fruit-scented
Survivor-wise
Head filled with pride.
Pinned down now
Rising.
Keen as a chiselling
Wind you erode my naiveties
Clear paths to new possibilities.
Beneath lust's torrential rush

A more abiding current stirs.

But I step away.

Belying your negritude
Lies a constant question
Am I your golden, granite Barack Obama?
Your courageous Martin Luther?
Or the man who split your lip
When white men were out of reach
Who pawned your pride and his own
For childish whims and tricks
Who let life exploding within him implode
Who found home on street corners?

I move to answer, but turn to stone.
In truth I don't know.

3
Like a fairytale turned on its head
You rest in a glass grave
Close enough to kiss, distant as a star.
I spin yarns to leave you a trail
But my tales are the stock of common shocks

I have no history of continents criss-crossed
· Of cartoon courage and cruelty
And I lack the tongue to season the sagas
With which you once bewitched me.
I cannot tempt you home.

I quest for a key to unlock
The spell, but now in crisis
Am without allies; and curse the
Coolness between our kith and kith
Cultivated by mutual consent.

Like the folded arm and crooked finger
Of the three ugly sisters
Banished doubts begin to bait:
'Tut tut three brown babies and no ring'
'Sad deluded sex tourist.'
I begin to falter and wonder
If the whispers have weight.
Am I witch or heroine?

After every fruitless foray I return
Less certain. Without animation
You become more alien
And I begin to wish you never wake.

Holy War

In the bazaar another blast, dust and wailing, limbless listless
  surrender.
Latest horror in the chronicle of Holy War: others before:
Unwilling martyrs subsumed in the Twin Towers spectacular.
Carriages in carnage heat and melted steel in Europe's heartlands.
Tears in Pakistan for hope's harbinger killed on the cusp of a new
  dawn.
For what cause, for what creed do men and women bayonet the
  youngest seed?
I add my voice to the clamour against Jihadist monsters.
But what of the architects of my own liberty?
Maroon Nanny who slew the fearful to harden the faithful when
  fleeing British fire.
Dessalines whose rebel army on route to Haiti's trumpeted victory
Cut down every white upon sight and piled the bodies without
  ceremony.
Prophet Turner who crushed the skulls of innocent and offender in
  Old Virginia.
What of every slave who bit and bit back until endurance finally
  broke.
Who, sanctified by suffering, took on the strength and surety of demi-
  Gods,
To release a total reckoning upon a foe marked for the most part by
  colour.
Ideas and eras shade yet the drama remains unchanged: history
  repeats as tragedy without farce.
I pause: am I part of an implacable order and today's assassins
  freedom fighters.

Choked

Hubris brings me home,
The prodigal restored.
I kneel: the miracle chokes
Like coal-lined lungs.

Chalk white, peace warrior,
Spat-upon 'nigger lover',
Model of messiah love,
Man of God I love,
You are the dam.

I fear the acid imprint
Of a Judas Kiss,
See fork-tongued midwives
To parasitic mission, ancestors
Lost in a smog of incense.

The wafer quivers upon
My tongue. Becomes a slurry.
Dissolves.
Void.

The Coat of Many Colours

She spins at her machine
A coat of rainbow colours
To cover the gaping wounds
Left by callous lovers.

She is a peacock on public display
Shunned for breaking the code of the flock
Yet secretly revered for sound advice
When troubles come.

Her eldest born beaten daily
By the vicious chirrup of fellow starlings.
And toothless crows cannot conceive
Her couture is an act of surgery
Offering their fragile nest a modicum of security
Convinced the coat's a callous
Assault upon their fledgling dignity.
They plot against the machine.

The nest divides upon age lines
The elders remember a time
Before the curse of Many Colours
Of a suitably invisible mother
The chicks knowing no better
Are inured to the Colours.

The coats are cast upon a pyre
And we child dissenters
Wished that they like
Meshach, Shadrach and Abednego
Would not burn.

Roughly uncovered
Her wounds seep openly
That regret cannot heal
Her broken song becomes one
Long scream
Our fragile nest burns with the machine.

Come

When Marcia Wine

Is like de worl fall wey
Man trouble, oman trouble
Money trouble, pickney trouble
No ave no weight
When she a wine.

Oman a watch wid green eye
Man a step to she
Fa de bump and grin
De grey head dem get misty eye
A rewin time but she
Nar pay dem nar min
When she a wine.

Stone heart man
Blood pressure rise
Herbsman lay down im pipe
And start fly pon de vibe
Even pastor start fantasize
When she a wine.

People wid 2 lef feet
Start to step to 2 beat
Sway dem hip, an fling
Dem body til dem get weak.
When she a wine.

She is de centre of we solar system
We Cinderella who no need no slipper
A catwalk queen wid full body
Black and roun she nar check skin bleach or chicken feed.
She battle scar is we history.
Marcia dance fa she fa everybody.

Me hear pon de ghetto vine
Marcia ketch she dream
An a dance pon TV

But when mi si down
Me a wonder wha mi a see
It come like dem chop Marcia inna t'ree
She leg, she breas
But mos mi see is one big batty
A fill up de screen.
Mi no see no Marcia
De oman who use fe wine
An mek everybody feel Irie.

Inner City Addictions

Debris from a cold coupling
Lies curled like a shrivelled worm
Amongst the common brilliance
Of bright-faced daisies.

The siren's screech
Mingles with Motown harmonies
Floating from the an Old Anansi's radio
His gift to the street.

Stark against the sombre
Chic of the many that
Survive daily attrition,
A lost prophet drowns in dreams
And screams to quiet demons.

Once thriving temple
Now silent sandstone husk
Bestrides the horizon
While towering hymns proclaiming New Jerusalems
Resound from cramped basements.

Lemon yellow, tangerine
Universal Empire, World, Rajah Stores
Face lurking furtive gangs
Racing in and out of the Underworld.

Smoking cars smoulder
Savaged in joyous revenge
Against an imagined gentry
Dumped beside ritually cleaned automobiles.

Chemical migrants search
For synthetic asylums
While the frantic inventions
Of the young at play
Subvert a landscape of decay.

High upon voyeurism
My inner city addiction
I apprehend nothing more
Than the cell of my own Soul.

Sweet Sixteen

What is sweet for this sixteen
Sucking dicks of nameless tricks
Down dead-end alleyways

She is a survivor
Orphaned in a peacetime country
The streets have become mother and father
But her sisters
There are plenty
In every ghetto in every city
From Bristol to Jo'burg

And brothers
He
Smooth-tongued snake-hearted
Took her under
His broken vulture's wing

Taught terror from a paternal tyrant
Has learnt to despise
Woman-hate eats
Away his insides

But when bruising exposed the lie
A matchmaker found her
A more exacting lover
Capable like a divine
To metamorphosis

He first appeared as a white line
And as her love grew
Crystallized into a rock
Neatly wrapped up
In a suit of shining armour

Heaven is the rush
Up the white aisle
Bells singing
To the ooooooooooo zone
Of their reunion
Before
Crashing down
To a new ending.

Loving him has made
Her smile a broken window
Her skin a battle ground
And inside sleeps an infection
The incubation of a doomsday child.

Rescued

I am spilling
Back into life
Slowly setting
Like ink spreading
Over tissue paper.
Rescued from slippage
By tiny hands, unbroken voices.
Their demands are anchors
Tears to dry
Quarrels to quash
Ears and eyes to inspect
Stomachs to fill.
Evening: we huddle
Together shutting
Out the wilderness
I cling to them: them to me.

Possession

If I press here
Drag a quite blade
Along tightened skin
Reach deeply, dive
And carve a precise line
I might let him out.

Somehow beneath the plum
Blueberry and cherry pastel
He gnaws his returns
But if I press here…

Come

I

Merman

Walk with me little one
Past the red brick rows
Across the smart green
Cut through the
Jangled hedge, wind round

The willow-draped bank
Pause a while to admire the
Navy blue dragonflies
Skitter over the still water.

Walk with me little one
Along the rust and weed
Rambled track, pass walls
Tagged in bright and humble
Scrawl.

Scramble down the
Jagged bank beneath
The churned flyover
To the crossroads.

Walk with me little one
Down the track
Where thorns protrude
Like fishing hooks,
Nettles rise up and bite.

Count the doves spotted along the
Muddy banks of the estuary, little one,
Take in the imperious walls of the gorge.
Then let us plunge into the wild beyond.

Inhale summer little one
For the last time. In the
Copse a forgotten corner
A perfect makeshift altar.
A killing time finally
Mine.

Little black Sambo
Of dog-dumb trust
Barrel-nosed big jubba lipped
Stitched and ripped.
Filthy underside of black pride
You must die.

I hack, slash, stab
Splash in gore and guts
Yet after every bloody thrill
You return a merman
Monster. Invincible unstoppable.

II

Mama Wata

I slip, watch the dust sparkle
Sparkle and let the demons
Gnaw my guts. Another one
for the ward. Saved.

Dreadlock, alto
You came: water spirit
In fragile form.
Opened ear then heart
To arrest an unknowable
Fall. I float back to life.
But I could not pull you ashore
Your current too strong.
Somewhere you flail against the tide.

III

Flux and fever ridden
Startled blinking
Bile-caked, beaten
By sun gloating
Black flower embossed
Upon charred tree, bitter
Sweet birthing of black child
Vexed head emerging
Shade in prayer, flight in dance
Abrupt ending, whip
Outrunning oceans
Striving, striving
England yearning turning
To fury spiralling
Capsizing into glory
Found in guns and gold,
Emblem encased ebbing:
Street killing.
I am encircled by Ancestors
Living and departed,
Chanting circling, pressing,

I open every pore
To imbibe their:
Sorrow wisdom,
Ruinous secrets
Scraps of melody,
Frayed lexicons
Grasped scraps
Of motherland
Ballast seed and sand
Cells to knowing
Last cries lost rites.

I take my place
Amongst the circle
Become part of their
Continuum.

Possibilities of Love
or Possibilities of Love Between Prospero and Caliban

How can you love me
Knowing I will do what you will not
Wipe away the shit and sick
Of your first and second childhood
Spit and shine your shoes
Sweep the muck caked streets
That belong to you.

How can you love me
When l come to you
Mute and pliant like meat
My bones sighing from years of service.
How can you love me
When those years have left me in penury
And l and my progeny
Hang upon your mercy.

How can you love me
When your arts are my guide and textbook
When l am a doll dancing to your tune.

If l become you
Use your words with precise diction
Speak your words with exact enunciation
Eat sleep walk dream as you do
Kill my Gods in the name of love
For those you have in pity bestowed
Perhaps then you will love me
But I do not think so.

Perhaps you will love me
When you see me not as you
When you see me black bold and free
When I tame your savage wisdom revive
The embers of ancestral memory
And re-imagine me
When you see that I see your heart
Shrunken and shrill as the shrew

And I extend my gourd to you
Which is full with the fruits of joy and sorrow
And you eat and weep with release
Freed from the need to be Caliban
Perhaps then you may love me
And more perhaps then I will love you.

Play It Again Sam

'Play it again Sam'
Fed on the milk of fame
Sam is a pipe,
To be played
Under the spotlight.

Sam bursts into thundering
Baritone princely falsetto
The velvet tones of Nat King Cole
Under the spotlight.

He smiles a Cab Calloway smile
Jitterbugs and jives,
Tip, tap scats
With feet and tongue
To the beat of a buried drum.

Sam slides like JB
Blaspheming
Against gravity
Spins, locks
Moon walks
Rolls rocks and rocks
Under the spotlight.

Sam can
Punch, kick
Leap, backflip
Hop, skip, jump
Triple jump
Into legend
Under the spotlight.

Sam is oozing
Like Ali against Foreman
Looking to the corner
Longing for the darkness beyond.
But fears death by anonymity.
Circumscribed.
Under the spotlight.

Sam beholds his plight:
The spotlight is an evil eye
A torturer's lamp to kill by.
Sam hones his mind and fists into
Weapons of resistance.

White hot oratory
Marching for humanity
Burning the innards of cities
Reduced to TV ratings
Under the spotlight.

Now locked in open struggle
The spotlight reveals its true guise:
Massa's voice, a whip
And wicked hands
An incubus slurping
Up his soul
Screaming:
'Dance, boy
Sing, boy
Strut, boy
Rage, boy
Holler
Hate
Cry, boy, cry.'

Faced with the abyss
Sam dives into darkness.
Applause is replaced by
Hiss and boos, and
A rainfall of rotting vegetables
But in the dark
Sam can sing
Shadow box
And boogey to his own tune.
Never to play it again
Under the spotlight.

Insect Cleansing

It is a 352 day battle
Dissecting wood lice
With hair dryers
Gingerly plucking limbs
From crane flies.
Performing the martial art
Of insect swatting
Luring wasps to certain
Death by Carlsberg
Lining doors with table salt
And planting lemon rinds
To kill invisible vermin.

If nature and alchemy do not suffice
We turn to chemical warfare
Vim, Ajax, Dettol
And the final solution Domestos.

It is a losing battle:
Soggy nights bring the slow invasion
Of slugs pouring boneless bodies through fissures
The map of their visitation mock our defences
Our intimate spaces are ecologies
And we ingest and egest bacterium.

My Simple Plea

De greatest threat to British identity
Is not de
African
Asian
Eastern European
Not even devolution
But becoming American.

Mi haf fe sey
Ow it puzzle mi
Mi parents come ere
When Inglan was de Queen
And we country was colony
But right ya now
It com in like Inglan is colony
An America is Mudder Country.

It started slowly:
As a chil I remember Wimpy
But now everybody wan fe yam McDs an KFC
Mi did look forward to wearin
Mi kilt and tweed but look now
Everybody a fight fe fit
Into American fashion.

We use fe buy locally
Doing our bit fa de lan of ope and glory
But now everybody a go outa town
And de local shops get bruk down.

Now some a we a call each other niggas and bitches
Like dats something good to be.
Come in like dem forget how we fight
To be called Human Being.
Dem a drop to gangster rap
When calyspo was de original
Political street poetry
An a act like dem in Harlem, Washington
- or West Kingston - now dat is a whole different story -

When dey is in London, Bristol, Birmingham.
All dis because of the madness
Coming from TV.

Nothing wrong with r'n'b,
Otis, Aretha and Stevie
Can inspire dey cyant sing
De story of we street so big up
So big up all who mek Inglan
The well of their creativity.

Some activist can quote every word
From Malcolm X biography
Dem can even tell yu de content
Of Martin Luther King las meal.
But who know bout Clau-de-ya Jones
Lawd Pitt an Harold Moody?
We have a history right here
We have our own revolutionaries.

But what hope have we
When we politicians sell de country
Cross de sea fe mek lickle money
Yet bawl bout immigration and refugee
An we prime minister (should l say President)
- TB, GB, soon to be DC - is part of a dynasty
That bow to de yankee.

My simple plea:
It not about integration or assimilation
It's something far more funky
It's a joy fe mix up ackee
Wid cottage cheese
Nyam roti wid fry dumplin
Eat fofo and baked beans.

We mek a new language
Add Yard talk and Punjabi
To Cockney, Brummie
And West Country.
An if we buk up on the Queen
We can still soun like the BBC.

So whether yu tink
Inglan is a Bitch
Bablyon, the Mother Country
Or a land of milk and honey
Stop a while, turn off the TV
Listen to the symphony
Of the inner city:
The Allah Akbar in melody
With Oh Happy Day.
The tabla fusing with the Tambourine
De sound clash between
Bhangra and D'n'B
Children of all colours
Singing old sea shanties.
Britain is a meeting place
Where African, Caribbean, Asian and Chinese
Can creole a new Soul.

So if we must import
Show a little positive discrimination
Buy the good seed
Not de bad weed
Or else stick wid de homegrown.

But if we don't check we
We will be nothing but facsimiles
Of a country where many are not free.

Transformed

Grey grandmother, grey father,
Rise out of the rocking chair,
Worn mother, worn father,
Lift up your veil and dream,
Child cast away the cool
That smothers your shine,
Brother, sister, turn off the money clock
Pastor, bury the sermon
On Sodom and Gommorah.

Rude bwoy, rude girl, settle.
Strip away the scars of yesterday
The binds of today,
The millstones of tomorrow,
Come play.

Put on your sequins, pearls, Nikes,
Bikinis and thongs,
Anoint with Old Spice and Christian Dior,
Adorn with glitter, gold, and gleaming stones
Grow giant wings, limbs, tusks, claws,
Wrap in jungle fur, and futuristic foil,
Cast a loving eye over the masquerade,
Embrace friend and foe in meaningless conversation.

Drink the sound, the drum heartbeat
That in driven wind, biting cold, warms,
Jump wine whistle wave
Bop to the boom of the Big Bass Speaker
Move with slow regality.
Taste the sizzle of juice dripping chicken,
Ram up on mango, melon, corn,
Reel with the rush of white rum.
Wade in the water where, ancestors, Orisha, God dwell
- Human and divine woven into One -
Fly to worlds beyond.
On this day.
On this day be
Transformed.

Iris and Edith

You would never believe
Iris and Edith use to be sworn enemies.
After Iris move into Edith street in 1960,
"They'll bring down de area
Wid dere rice and peas and prayer meetings,"
Edith would scream.
While Iris would tell she frien
Dem "de people to-ta-lee ungodly."
It comin like World War T'ree
Wid Iris a represent Black Power
And Edith de Keep Britain White party.

Now Iris husban John
Sey im wan bring peace to everyone.
So im couldn't understan why Devon cuss his R & C
After im ask, all speaky spokey,
"If Black people ave tail like monkey?"

The pressure ease
After Iris ave her first pickney
And Edith couldn't help but scream:
"What a beauty!"
Though in she heart she was glad
It wasn't a brown baby.
After that dem resume hostilities.

Til one afternoon Edith shock
To see Devon a sprint like athlete.
She was gi bawl out "Stop tief!"
Til she see im was chase by three Teddies.
Iris fling open de door
Devon dive inside: a second later
An im would a meet im maker.

Now Edith never like black
But she couldn't abide dat.
She Daddy died in de blitz
An fa dat she hate Fascist.

She cool she fire an over de
Fence would share a cuppa.
You could even ketch er
Humming Desmond Dekker.
Edith had to admit Iris and her family were decent
 - Well for coloured folk.

But dat idea she come to forfeit
When she get invite to dem wedding.
Edith felt like cruff when she
De folks all dress up
De oman like Grace Kelly
De men like Al Capone, Cagney
Ey one Jamaican even ketch er fancy.

Iris go Bingo to return de favour
But she never understan 'de fat lady' lingua.
The women found dey ad a common frien:
Edith call im Christ and visit im once a week;
Iris call im Jesus and was always at his feet.

It seem everyting was cook and curry
Afta dem both fin work
Inna de same tobacco factory.
But tings tek a reverse
When Iris big son and Edith big daughter announce they wan fe
marry.
Both mothers agree it would be a terrible ting
To ave mixed children.
"They sure dey would ave no identity."
In the end dem ave fe give in after
Dem fin out it was gi be a shotgun wedding.
From den on the two women purge
Dem differences to give dem Grandchil a dual heritage.

De learn bout each other history,
Bout de potato famine, bout slavery,
An outdo each udder cussing de British.

Edith learn fe cook bangers and ackee;
Iris a cottage pie wid curry mutton.

Dem draw closer still
After Devon die from cancer.
Straight after John up
An gone to Australia
To teach naked Yoga.

Wid no man in sight
De two woman start live
Dem life. Dem study everyting
From computing to boxercise.
An travel de world from Brazil to Mongolia.

De neighbourhood change
De ol timers pass away
De youngsters move on
De council tear down the slum
To mek high-rise version.

Iris and Edith
Hol de oral history
Of de street.
If yu pass dem yu would swear
Dem ave one body both intertwined like creeping vine
Over a tall oak tree.

On Glastonbury Tor

Sat upon the clay ground
They face each other
Like spirits born from the mist
That wreathes the land around
Dreadlocked Celt dreadlocked African

They once fodder for factories
Once beasts upon a whored paradise
Are now surplus to necessity:
The mills are empty
A ghastly perfect land
Needs no human hand

The Celt through his pipe
The African his drum
Ramble through ancient paths
Searching for mothering
Upon this trammled soil

Strangers at the crossroads of re-creation
The outcome uncertain
Will they come to a new understanding
Or repeat an endless cycle?